From
BURNOUT
to
BALANCE

Implementing Mindfulness
in Your Professional Life

LANCE J. MILES

FROM BURNOUT TO BALANCE

CONTENTS

Introduction 5

1. Understanding Burnout 10
2. Exploring the Neuroscience Behind Mindfulness 21
3. Getting Started with Mindfulness 37
4. Mindful Work Habits 56
5. Managing Stress and Anxiety 74
6. Enhancing Communication and Relationships 89
7. Work-Life Integration 102
8. Sustaining Your Mindfulness Practice 114

Introduction

In today's fast-paced and demanding work environment, the prevalence of burnout has become a significant concern for professionals across industries. Defined as a state of emotional, physical, and mental exhaustion caused by excessive and prolonged stress, burnout can have detrimental effects on individuals' well-being and productivity. It can manifest in various ways, including feelings of cynicism, detachment from work, and a sense of inefficacy. Left unchecked, burnout can not only impair job performance but also lead to serious health issues and negatively impact personal relationships.

The World Health Organization (WHO) has recognized burnout as an occupational phenomenon, highlighting its widespread prevalence and the need for effective strategies to address it. While organizational factors such as heavy workload, lack of autonomy, and poor work-life balance contribute to burnout, individuals also play a crucial role in managing their well-being and resilience in the face of workplace stressors.

In recent years, mindfulness has emerged as a

promising approach for combating burnout and promoting mental well-being in the workplace. Rooted in ancient contemplative traditions, mindfulness involves paying attention to the present moment with openness, curiosity, and acceptance. By cultivating awareness of our thoughts, feelings, and sensations without judgment, mindfulness enables individuals to respond to stressors with greater clarity, composure, and resilience.

This book, "From Burnout to Balance: Implementing Mindfulness in Your Professional Life," is designed to provide practical guidance and tools for integrating mindfulness practices into your daily work routine. Whether you're experiencing early signs of burnout or simply seeking to enhance your overall well-being and performance, this resource offers a comprehensive roadmap for navigating the challenges of the modern workplace with mindfulness.

Chapter Overview

The book is divided into eight chapters, each focusing on different aspects of mindfulness in the context of professional life. Here's an overview of what you can expect to find in each chapter:

Chapter 1: Understanding Burnout

In this chapter, we'll explore the concept of burnout in-depth, examining its causes, symptoms, and impact on professional performance. By gaining a deeper understanding of burnout, you'll be better equipped to recognize the signs and take proactive steps to address them.

Chapter 2: The Science of Mindfulness

Building on the foundation laid in the first chapter, we'll delve into the science behind mindfulness and its potential benefits for combating burnout. From the neuroscience of mindfulness to evidence-based research supporting its efficacy, this chapter will provide insights into why mindfulness is a powerful tool for promoting mental well-being.

Chapter 3: Getting Started with Mindfulness

If you're new to mindfulness or unsure where to

begin, this chapter is for you. We'll explore practical strategies for establishing a mindfulness practice, overcoming common challenges, and integrating mindfulness into your daily routine. Whether you have five minutes or an hour to spare, you'll learn how to make mindfulness a sustainable habit.

Chapter 4: Mindful Work Habits

In this chapter, we'll shift our focus to the workplace and explore how mindfulness can enhance your professional life. From techniques for staying focused and present during meetings to creating a mindful workspace environment, you'll discover practical tips for incorporating mindfulness into your work habits.

Chapter 5: Managing Stress and Anxiety

Workplace stress is a common trigger for burnout, but mindfulness can help you manage stress more effectively. In this chapter, we'll explore mindfulness tools and techniques for coping with workplace stressors, calming anxiety, and building resilience in the face of adversity.

Chapter 6: Enhancing Communication and Relationships

Effective communication and positive relationships are essential for a healthy work environment. In this chapter, we'll explore how mindfulness can improve your communication skills, deepen your connections with colleagues, and foster a culture of trust and collaboration in your workplace.

Chapter 7: Work-Life Integration

Achieving a healthy work-life balance is essential for preventing burnout and maintaining overall well-being. In this chapter, we'll discuss strategies for setting boundaries, prioritizing self-care, and integrating mindfulness into your personal life to achieve greater harmony and fulfillment.

Chapter 8: Sustaining Your Mindfulness Practice

Finally, in our last chapter, we'll focus on sustaining your mindfulness practice over the long term. From tips for maintaining consistency and motivation to overcoming setbacks and challenges, you'll learn how to cultivate a lifelong mindfulness habit that supports your well-being and resilience.

1. Understanding Burnout

Recognizing the Signs and Symptoms

In our modern, fast-paced world, the term "burnout" has become increasingly prevalent, often used to describe a state of chronic stress and exhaustion. Whether you're a seasoned professional or just starting your career journey, understanding the signs and symptoms of burnout is crucial for maintaining your well-being and performance in the workplace. In this subchapter, we'll delve into the nuanced signs and symptoms of burnout, exploring how they manifest in different aspects of our lives and work.

The Multifaceted Nature of Burnout

Burnout isn't a one-size-fits-all condition; rather, it's a complex interplay of physical, emotional, and mental exhaustion. Recognizing burnout requires a keen awareness of these various dimensions and how they manifest in our daily lives.

Physical Exhaustion: The Body's Cry for Rest

One of the most tangible manifestations of burnout is physical exhaustion. It's that bone-deep weariness that settles in, regardless of how much sleep you get or how many cups of coffee you down. Your body feels heavy, your muscles ache, and even the simplest tasks can feel like Herculean feats.

But physical exhaustion isn't just about feeling tired; it's about feeling depleted on a fundamental level. It's your body's way of telling you that it's reached its limit, that it can't keep up with the relentless demands being placed upon it. And if left unchecked, this physical exhaustion can have serious consequences for your health and well-being.

Emotional Exhaustion: The Weight of the World on Your Shoulders

Alongside physical exhaustion comes emotional exhaustion, a sense of being drained to the core. It's that feeling of running on empty, of having nothing left to give. You find yourself irritable, short-tempered, and emotionally volatile, snapping at colleagues, friends, and loved ones for the smallest infractions.

Emotional exhaustion can also manifest as a pervasive sense of numbness or apathy, where you find yourself going through the motions without any real sense of joy or passion. It's as if the color has drained from your life, leaving everything dull and lifeless in its wake.

Cognitive Exhaustion: When Your Brain

Hits a Brick Wall

In addition to physical and emotional exhaustion, burnout also takes a toll on your cognitive functioning. You find it increasingly difficult to concentrate, to stay focused on tasks, and to retain information. Your mind feels foggy, sluggish, and unresponsive, as if it's been wrapped in a thick blanket of cotton wool.

This cognitive exhaustion can have serious implications for your work performance, making it harder to meet deadlines, solve problems, and make decisions. You find yourself making careless mistakes, overlooking important details, and struggling to keep up with the demands of your job.

Behavioral Changes: When Burnout Starts to Show Its Face

As burnout takes its toll, you may also notice changes in your behavior. You become more withdrawn and socially isolated, retreating into yourself as a way of coping with the overwhelming demands of your life. You may also turn to unhealthy coping mechanisms, such as excessive drinking, smoking, or overeating, as a way of numbing the pain and stress.

At the same time, you may also become more cynical and detached, adopting a "what's the point?" attitude towards your work and your life. You no longer derive any real sense of satisfaction or fulfillment from what you do, seeing it as nothing more than a means to an end.

The Importance of Self-Awareness: Listening to Your Body, Mind, and Spirit

In the midst of all this turmoil, it's easy to lose sight of yourself, to become so caught up in the chaos of your life that you forget to listen to your body, mind, and spirit. But self-awareness is the key to recognizing burnout before it spirals out of control, to taking proactive steps to address it before it takes over your life.

So take the time to check in with yourself on a regular basis. Pay attention to how you're feeling physically, emotionally, and mentally. Notice any changes or shifts in your mood, energy levels, or behavior. And if you start to notice any signs or symptoms of burnout, don't ignore them. Reach out for support, whether it's from friends, family, or a professional, and take the steps necessary to reclaim your well-being and balance.

The Impact of Burnout on Professional Performance

In today's fast-paced and demanding work environments, burnout has emerged as a significant threat to professional performance. Beyond its toll on personal well-being, burnout can have profound implications for productivity, creativity, and overall effectiveness in the workplace. In this subchapter, we'll explore how burnout affects professional performance and why addressing it is crucial for both individuals and organizations.

The Cycle of Burnout: A Vicious Spiral

At its core, burnout is a vicious cycle fueled by chronic stress, exhaustion, and disengagement. As individuals experience increasing levels of stress and pressure in the workplace, they may initially respond by working harder, pushing themselves to meet deadlines and achieve goals. However, as the demands continue to mount and resources become depleted, this relentless pursuit of productivity can quickly lead to burnout.

One of the key features of burnout is a sense of inefficacy or reduced accomplishment, where individuals feel like they're no longer able to meet the demands of their job or perform at their usual level of competence. This can manifest as decreased productivity, increased errors and mistakes, and a general sense of disengagement from work tasks.

Impaired Decision-Making and Problem-Solving

Burnout also takes a toll on cognitive functioning, impairing individuals' ability to think clearly, make decisions, and solve problems effectively. When you're feeling mentally exhausted and overwhelmed, it's much harder to focus attention, process information, and weigh the pros and cons of different courses of action.

As a result, individuals experiencing burnout may find themselves making poor decisions, overlooking important details, and struggling to find creative solutions to problems. This can have serious implications for job performance, particularly in roles that require complex decision-making and problem-solving skills.

Decline in Creativity and Innovation

In addition to impaired decision-making, burnout can also stifle creativity and innovation in the workplace. When you're feeling emotionally and mentally drained, it's much harder to think outside the box, generate new ideas, and approach challenges from a fresh perspective.

As a result, individuals experiencing burnout may find themselves stuck in a rut, relying on familiar solutions and approaches rather than exploring new possibilities. This can hinder progress and innovation within organizations, stifling growth and competitiveness in an increasingly dynamic and fast-paced business environment.

Strained Relationships and Collaboration

Burnout doesn't just affect individual performance; it can also strain relationships and collaboration within teams and organizations. When you're feeling exhausted, irritable, and disconnected from your work, it's much harder to communicate effectively, resolve conflicts, and collaborate with colleagues.

As a result, workplace relationships may suffer, leading to tension, resentment, and breakdowns in communication. This can undermine teamwork and cooperation, making it harder to achieve common goals and objectives within the organization.

Increased Absenteeism and Turnover

Finally, burnout can also contribute to increased absenteeism and turnover in the workplace. When individuals are feeling overwhelmed and exhausted, they may be more likely to call in sick or take time off to recover. Similarly, if burnout persists unchecked, individuals may ultimately decide to leave their job in search of a healthier and more fulfilling work environment.

This can have serious implications for organizations, leading to higher recruitment and training costs, decreased morale and productivity, and a loss of institutional knowledge and expertise. In the long run, addressing burnout isn't just about supporting individual well-being; it's also about safeguarding the health and performance of the organization as a whole.

Strategies for Prevention

As the old adage goes, "an ounce of prevention is worth a pound of cure." This sentiment holds particularly true when it comes to burnout. Rather than waiting until you're already in the throes of exhaustion and overwhelm, it's far more effective to take proactive steps to prevent burnout from occurring in the first place. In this subchapter, we'll explore a range of strategies for preventing burnout and promoting well-being and resilience in the workplace.

1. Cultivate Self-Awareness

The first step in preventing burnout is cultivating self-awareness. Pay attention to how you're feeling physically, emotionally, and mentally on a regular basis. Notice any signs or symptoms of stress and exhaustion, such as fatigue, irritability, or difficulty concentrating. By tuning into your body and mind, you can identify early warning signs of burnout and take proactive steps to address them before they escalate.

2. Set Boundaries

One of the most common contributors to burnout is a lack of boundaries between work and personal life. In today's hyper-connected world, it's all too easy to blur the lines between work and leisure, checking emails late into the night or working through weekends. However, this constant availability can take a toll on your well-being, leaving you feeling exhausted and overwhelmed.

To prevent burnout, it's important to set clear boundaries around your work and personal life. Establish designated work hours and stick to them as much as possible. Turn off email notifications outside of work hours and resist the urge to check your work email or messages during leisure time. By creating space for rest and relaxation, you can recharge your batteries and prevent burnout from taking hold.

3. Practice Stress Management Techniques

Stress is a natural part of life, but chronic stress can quickly lead to burnout if left unchecked. To prevent burnout, it's important to develop healthy coping mechanisms for managing stress effectively. This may include practices such as mindfulness meditation, deep breathing exercises, yoga, or progressive muscle relaxation.

Find what works best for you and incorporate it into your daily routine. Taking just a few minutes each day to engage in stress-relieving activities can make a world of difference in preventing burnout and promoting well-being.

4. Prioritize Self-Care

Self-care is often the first thing to go when we're feeling stressed and overwhelmed, but it's also one of the most important tools for preventing burnout. Make self-care a priority in your daily life by engaging in activities that nourish your body, mind, and spirit.

This could be anything from taking a long bath, going for a walk in nature, reading a book, or spending time with loved ones. The key is to find activities that help you relax, recharge, and reconnect with yourself, allowing you to maintain a sense of balance and well-being in the face of life's challenges.

5. Build a Support System

When it comes to preventing burnout, social support is essential. Surround yourself with friends, family, and colleagues who lift you up and support you in times of need. Reach out to others when you're feeling stressed or overwhelmed, and don't be afraid to ask for help when you need it.

Building a strong support system can help buffer against the negative effects of stress and burnout, providing a sense of connection, belonging, and validation. Whether it's a listening ear, a shoulder to cry on, or practical assistance with tasks, having a support system in place can make all the difference in preventing burnout and promoting well-being.

6. Practice Mindfulness

Mindfulness is a powerful tool for preventing burnout by helping you stay present, focused, and resilient in the face of stress. Incorporate mindfulness practices into your daily routine, such as mindfulness meditation, mindful breathing, or body scan exercises.

By cultivating present-moment awareness and acceptance, mindfulness can help you respond to stressors with greater clarity, composure, and resilience. It can also help you appreciate the small joys and moments of beauty in your day-to-day life, fostering a sense of gratitude and well-being that acts as a buffer against burnout.

2. Exploring the Neuroscience Behind Mindfulness

Understanding the Brain's Response to Stress

To comprehend the neuroscience behind mindfulness, it's crucial to first grasp how the brain responds to stress. When faced with stressors, whether they're external challenges or internal worries, the brain initiates a series of physiological and psychological responses aimed at protecting the body and mind.

At the heart of the brain's stress response system is the amygdala, an almond-shaped structure located deep within the brain's temporal lobe. The amygdala acts as the brain's alarm system, detecting potential threats in the environment and triggering the body's fight-or-flight response. When the amygdala perceives a threat, it sends signals to the hypothalamus, which activates the sympathetic nervous system, leading to the release of stress hormones like cortisol and adrenaline.

These stress hormones prepare the body for action, increasing heart rate, blood pressure, and respiration rate to help us respond to the perceived threat. However, prolonged exposure to stress can dysregulate this system, leading to chronic activation of the stress response and contributing to the development of conditions like anxiety, depression, and burnout.

The Role of the Prefrontal Cortex in Emotion Regulation

In addition to the amygdala, another key player in the brain's stress response system is the prefrontal cortex, the region of the brain responsible for higher-order cognitive functions such as decision-making, impulse control, and emotion regulation. The prefrontal cortex plays a crucial role in modulating the activity of the amygdala and dampening the stress response.

However, under conditions of chronic stress, the prefrontal cortex can become impaired, leading to deficits in emotion regulation and cognitive control. This can manifest as difficulty concentrating, making decisions, and managing emotions effectively, further exacerbating the cycle of stress and contributing to the development of mental health problems like anxiety and depression.

The Neuroscience of Mindfulness: A New Perspective

In recent years, neuroscientists have begun to explore the effects of mindfulness on the brain, shedding light on the underlying mechanisms by which mindfulness practices can modulate the stress response and promote emotional well-being. One area of particular interest is the impact of mindfulness on the structure and function of the brain's stress response system.

Research using neuroimaging techniques such as functional magnetic resonance imaging (fMRI) and electroencephalography (EEG) has revealed that mindfulness practices can lead to changes in the structure and function of key brain regions involved in emotion regulation, including the prefrontal cortex and the amygdala. For example, studies have shown that regular mindfulness meditation can increase gray matter density in the prefrontal cortex, strengthening its ability to regulate emotions and control impulses.

Furthermore, mindfulness has been found to reduce activity in the amygdala, dampening the brain's response to stress and promoting a greater sense of calm and equanimity. This downregulation of the amygdala is thought to be mediated by changes in connectivity between the prefrontal cortex and the amygdala, resulting in more adaptive responses to stressful situations.

The Role of the Default Mode Network in Mindfulness

Another brain network that has garnered attention in mindfulness research is the default mode network (DMN), a network of brain regions involved in self-referential thinking, mind-wandering, and rumination. When the DMN is active, we tend to be lost in thought, ruminating on the past or worrying about the future.

Mindfulness practices have been found to modulate activity in the DMN, leading to reduced rumination and increased present-moment awareness. This shift in brain activity is thought to underlie many of the cognitive and emotional benefits of mindfulness, including reduced stress, improved mood, and enhanced well-being.

The Body's Response to Stress

Stress is an inherent part of life, eliciting a complex physiological response that prepares the body to face perceived threats or challenges. Understanding the intricate interplay between the brain, nervous system, and hormonal pathways during times of stress is essential for comprehending the profound impact it can have on our physical and mental well-being.

The Stress Response: Fight or Flight

At the core of the body's response to stress lies the sympathetic nervous system, often referred to as the "fight or flight" response. When faced with a stressor, whether it's a looming deadline or an unexpected crisis, the brain's amygdala sends signals to the hypothalamus, triggering the release of stress hormones such as adrenaline and cortisol.

These hormones act on various organs and tissues throughout the body, initiating a cascade of physiological changes designed to enhance our ability to respond to the threat. Heart rate and blood pressure increase, diverting blood flow away from non-essential functions like digestion and towards muscles and organs involved in physical exertion. Meanwhile, respiration rate increases, ensuring a steady supply of oxygen to the brain and muscles.

The Role of Cortisol: The Body's Stress Hormone

Cortisol, often referred to as the body's primary stress hormone, plays a central role in orchestrating the stress response. Released by the adrenal glands in response to signals from the hypothalamus and pituitary gland, cortisol helps regulate metabolism, immune function, and the body's response to stress.

In the short term, cortisol serves a vital function, mobilizing energy stores and enhancing cognitive function to help us cope with immediate threats. However, prolonged exposure to high levels of cortisol can have detrimental effects on health, contributing to a range of problems such as impaired immune function, weight gain, and increased risk of chronic diseases like diabetes and heart disease.

The HPA Axis: The Stress Response System

The body's stress response is regulated by a complex feedback loop known as the hypothalamic-pituitary-adrenal (HPA) axis. When the brain perceives a stressor, the hypothalamus releases corticotropin-releasing hormone (CRH), which signals the pituitary gland to release adrenocorticotropic hormone (ACTH). ACTH, in turn, stimulates the adrenal glands to release cortisol, initiating the stress response.

This finely tuned system allows the body to mount an appropriate response to stressors while also preventing excessive activation of the stress response system. However, chronic stress can dysregulate the HPA axis, leading to prolonged elevation of cortisol levels and increasing the risk of health problems.

The Impact of Chronic Stress on Health

While the stress response is essential for survival, chronic activation of the stress response system can have serious consequences for health and well-being. Prolonged exposure to high levels of cortisol and other stress hormones can weaken the immune system, disrupt sleep patterns, and contribute to the development of a range of health problems, including:

- Cardiovascular disease: Chronic stress is a significant risk factor for hypertension, heart disease, and stroke, as it can lead to elevated blood pressure, inflammation, and arterial stiffness.
- Metabolic disorders: High levels of cortisol can disrupt insulin sensitivity, leading to insulin resistance, weight gain, and an increased risk of type 2 diabetes.
- Mental health disorders: Chronic stress is strongly linked to the development of anxiety disorders, depression, and other mood disorders, as it can disrupt neurotransmitter balance and impair cognitive function.

Understanding the Relationship Between Mindfulness and Burnout

In the face of ever-increasing demands and pressures in the modern workplace, burnout has become a prevalent issue affecting individuals across various professions. However, emerging research suggests that mindfulness practices offer a powerful antidote to burnout, providing individuals with the tools to cultivate resilience, well-being, and balance in the face of stressors. In this subchapter, we'll explore the relationship between mindfulness and burnout, examining how mindfulness practices can mitigate the risk of burnout and promote greater resilience in the workplace.

The Roots of Burnout: A Crisis of Modern Work

Before delving into the role of mindfulness in combatting burnout, it's essential to understand the underlying factors contributing to burnout in the workplace. Burnout often arises from a combination of prolonged stress, excessive workload, lack of autonomy, and a mismatch between an individual's values and the demands of their job. In today's fast-paced, hyper-connected work environments, individuals are constantly bombarded with emails, meetings, and deadlines, leaving little time for rest, relaxation, and self-care.

As a result, many individuals find themselves feeling overwhelmed, exhausted, and disconnected from their work, leading to a sense of disillusionment and burnout. Left unchecked, burnout can have serious consequences for both individuals and organizations, affecting job performance, job satisfaction, and overall well-being.

The Role of Mindfulness in Burnout Prevention

Mindfulness, rooted in ancient contemplative traditions such as meditation and yoga, offers a holistic approach to managing stress and promoting well-being. At its core, mindfulness involves paying attention to the present moment with openness, curiosity, and acceptance, without judgment or attachment. By cultivating awareness of our thoughts, feelings, and sensations, mindfulness enables individuals to respond to stressors with greater clarity, equanimity, and resilience.

Research has shown that mindfulness practices can mitigate the risk of burnout by:

- **Reducing Stress Reactivity**: Mindfulness practices help individuals become more aware of their stress responses and develop healthier ways of coping with stress. By cultivating a sense of presence and non-reactivity, mindfulness enables individuals to step back from automatic stress reactions and respond to stressors with greater calmness and clarity.

- **Enhancing Emotional Regulation**: One of the hallmarks of burnout is emotional exhaustion, characterized by feelings of depletion and disengagement. Mindfulness practices help individuals develop greater emotional regulation skills, allowing them to recognize and respond to emotions more skillfully. By cultivating a sense of equanimity and acceptance, mindfulness enables individuals to navigate challenging emotions without becoming overwhelmed or reactive.
- **Promoting Self-Compassion**: Burnout often arises from a sense of perfectionism and self-criticism, where individuals push themselves to meet unrealistic standards and berate themselves for falling short. Mindfulness practices promote self-compassion by encouraging individuals to approach themselves with kindness and understanding. By cultivating self-compassion, individuals can develop

greater resilience in the face of setbacks and challenges.
- **Fostering Resilience**: At its core, burnout is a manifestation of depleted resilience, where individuals feel unable to cope with the demands of their work and life. Mindfulness practices help individuals cultivate resilience by enhancing their ability to bounce back from adversity and adapt to change. By developing a greater sense of presence, purpose, and connection, mindfulness enables individuals to weather the storms of life with greater ease and grace.

The Evidence Base for Mindfulness and Burnout

The effectiveness of mindfulness in combatting burnout is supported by a growing body of scientific research. Numerous studies have demonstrated that mindfulness-based interventions can reduce symptoms of burnout, improve well-being, and enhance job satisfaction among individuals in various professions, including healthcare, education, and business.

For example, a meta-analysis published in the Journal of Occupational Health Psychology found that mindfulness-based interventions were associated with significant reductions in burnout and psychological distress among healthcare professionals. Similarly, a study published in the Journal of Occupational and Environmental Medicine found that mindfulness training led to improvements in burnout, stress, and job satisfaction among employees in a large healthcare organization.

Understanding the Research Landscape

In recent years, there has been a surge of interest in mindfulness practices and their potential benefits for mental health and well-being. Researchers have conducted numerous studies to investigate the effects of mindfulness on various aspects of psychological functioning, from stress reduction to emotional regulation to cognitive performance. In this subchapter, we'll explore the evidence-based benefits of mindfulness practices, drawing upon research from psychology, neuroscience, and medicine.

Stress Reduction and Resilience

One of the most well-documented benefits of mindfulness practices is their ability to reduce stress and enhance resilience in the face of adversity. Studies have consistently found that mindfulness-based interventions, such as mindfulness meditation and mindfulness-based stress reduction (MBSR), can lead to significant reductions in self-reported stress and physiological markers of stress, such as cortisol levels.

For example, a meta-analysis published in the Journal of Psychosomatic Research found that mindfulness-based interventions were associated with medium to large reductions in perceived stress across a variety of populations, including clinical and non-clinical samples. Similarly, a randomized controlled trial published in the Journal of Consulting and Clinical Psychology found that participants who completed an eight-week MBSR program reported greater reductions in perceived stress and greater improvements in coping strategies compared to a control group.

Emotional Regulation and Well-Being

Mindfulness practices have also been shown to enhance emotional regulation skills and promote greater well-being. By cultivating awareness of our thoughts, feelings, and sensations in the present moment, mindfulness enables individuals to respond to emotions with greater clarity, equanimity, and compassion.

Research has found that mindfulness-based interventions can lead to improvements in emotional regulation skills, such as decreased emotional reactivity, increased emotional awareness, and greater emotional resilience. For example, a study published in the journal Emotion found that participants who completed a brief mindfulness training program showed reduced emotional reactivity to negative stimuli compared to a control group.

Furthermore, numerous studies have demonstrated that mindfulness practices are associated with greater levels of well-being and life satisfaction. A meta-analysis published in the journal Psychological Bulletin found that mindfulness-based interventions were associated with small to moderate improvements in well-being across a variety of populations and settings.

Cognitive Functioning and Performance

In addition to its effects on stress and emotional well-being, mindfulness practices have also been shown to enhance cognitive functioning and performance. Research has found that mindfulness meditation can improve attention, concentration, working memory, and decision-making skills.

For example, a study published in the journal Psychological Science found that participants who completed a brief mindfulness training program showed improvements in attention and working memory compared to a control group. Similarly, a meta-analysis published in the journal Psychological Bulletin found that mindfulness-based interventions were associated with small to moderate improvements in cognitive performance across a variety of domains, including attention, memory, and executive function.

Physical Health and Immune Function

Beyond its effects on mental health and cognitive functioning, mindfulness practices have also been linked to improvements in physical health and immune function. Research has found that mindfulness-based interventions can lead to reductions in inflammation, blood pressure, and other markers of cardiovascular risk.

For example, a meta-analysis published in the journal JAMA Internal Medicine found that mindfulness-based interventions were associated with small to moderate reductions in blood pressure among individuals with hypertension. Similarly, a randomized controlled trial published in the journal Brain, Behavior, and Immunity found that participants who completed an eight-week MBSR program showed reductions in markers of inflammation compared to a control group.

3. Getting Started with Mindfulness

Establishing a Mindfulness Practice

Embarking on a journey to establish a mindfulness practice can be both exciting and challenging. It requires dedication, patience, and a willingness to cultivate awareness and presence in everyday life. In this chapter, we'll explore the various steps involved in establishing a mindfulness practice, from setting intentions to integrating mindfulness into daily routines.

Setting Intentions: Defining Your Why

Before diving into mindfulness practice, it's essential to clarify your intentions and motivations. Ask yourself: Why do you want to practice mindfulness? What do you hope to gain from it? Whether it's reducing stress, improving focus, or enhancing well-being, having a clear sense of purpose can help guide your practice and keep you motivated along the way.

Once you've identified your intentions, it can be helpful to write them down or create a personal mission statement to remind yourself of your goals. For example, you might write, "I practice mindfulness to cultivate greater peace and presence in my daily life."

Starting Small: Embracing Incremental Progress

When starting a mindfulness practice, it's tempting to dive in headfirst and attempt long meditation sessions or complex techniques. However, it's often more effective to start small and build momentum gradually. Begin with short, manageable sessions, such as five minutes of mindfulness meditation or a brief body scan exercise.

As you become more comfortable with these shorter practices, you can gradually increase the duration and complexity of your sessions. Remember, consistency is key. It's better to practice for a few minutes every day than to sporadically engage in longer sessions.

Finding Your Anchor: Choosing a Focus for Your Practice

In mindfulness practice, having a focal point or anchor can help anchor your attention and cultivate present-moment awareness. Common anchors include the breath, bodily sensations, sounds, or even a specific mantra or phrase.

Experiment with different anchors to see which resonates most with you.

For example, you might choose to focus on the sensation of the breath as it enters and leaves your nostrils, or the feeling of your feet making contact with the ground during a walking meditation. Find an anchor that feels comfortable and accessible, and use it as a point of reference to bring your attention back whenever it wanders.

Cultivating Non-Judgmental Awareness: Embracing Acceptance

A fundamental aspect of mindfulness is cultivating a non-judgmental attitude towards your thoughts, feelings, and experiences. Instead of reacting to them with aversion or attachment, practice observing them with curiosity and openness, allowing them to come and go without judgment.

For example, if you notice your mind wandering during meditation, instead of berating yourself for being distracted, simply acknowledge the distraction with kindness and gently guide your attention back to your chosen anchor. Over time, this practice of non-judgmental awareness can help cultivate greater self-compassion and resilience in the face of life's challenges.

Integrating Mindfulness into Daily Life: Bringing Awareness to Everyday Activities

While formal mindfulness meditation is an essential aspect of practice, true mindfulness extends beyond the meditation cushion and into everyday life. Look for opportunities to bring mindfulness to daily activities such as eating, walking, or even washing dishes.

For example, during mealtime, take a few moments to pause and fully savor each bite, noticing the flavors, textures, and sensations of the food. When walking, pay attention to the sensation of your feet touching the ground, the rhythm of your breath, and the sights and sounds around you. By integrating mindfulness into daily activities, you can cultivate greater presence and appreciation for the richness of each moment.

Creating a Supportive Environment: Cultivating Community and Accountability

Establishing a mindfulness practice can be challenging, especially when faced with distractions and competing priorities. Creating a supportive environment can help you stay on track and maintain consistency in your practice.

Consider joining a mindfulness group or community where you can connect with like-minded individuals, share experiences, and receive guidance and support. You can also enlist an accountability partner or mentor to help keep you motivated and accountable in your practice. By surrounding yourself with a supportive community, you can cultivate a sense of connection and belonging that enhances your mindfulness journey.

Reflecting on Your Practice: Cultivating Self-Awareness and Growth

Regularly reflecting on your mindfulness practice can deepen your self-awareness and facilitate personal growth. Take time to journal about your experiences, insights, and challenges, noting any patterns or themes that emerge.

For example, you might reflect on how your practice has influenced your mood, relationships, or decision-making processes. Notice any changes in your thoughts, feelings, or behaviors over time, and celebrate your progress, no matter how small. By cultivating a spirit of curiosity and inquiry, you can continue to evolve and deepen your mindfulness practice.

Overcoming Common Challenges

Navigating the path of mindfulness practice is not always smooth sailing. Like any journey, there are obstacles and challenges along the way that can hinder our progress and test our commitment. In this chapter, we'll explore some of the common challenges that arise in mindfulness practice and strategies for overcoming them.

1. Restlessness and Impatience

In our fast-paced world, cultivating mindfulness requires us to slow down and be present with whatever arises in the moment. However, many of us struggle with restlessness and impatience, constantly seeking distraction or stimulation to avoid sitting with uncomfortable thoughts or emotions.

To overcome restlessness and impatience in mindfulness practice, try incorporating periods of stillness and silence into your routine. Set aside time each day to simply be with your experience, without the need to do or achieve anything. Notice any impulses to distract yourself or escape from discomfort, and gently bring your attention back to the present moment.

2. Resistance and Avoidance

Resistance and avoidance are common barriers to mindfulness practice, particularly when it comes to facing difficult emotions or challenging situations. We may find ourselves avoiding meditation or mindfulness exercises because they bring up uncomfortable thoughts or feelings that we'd rather not confront.

Instead of avoiding difficult experiences, try leaning into them with a spirit of curiosity and compassion. Notice any resistance or aversion that arises and explore it with gentle curiosity. Remind yourself that discomfort is a natural part of the human experience and that by facing it directly, you can cultivate greater resilience and inner strength.

3. Self-Criticism and Judgement

Another common challenge in mindfulness practice is the tendency towards self-criticism and judgement. We may berate ourselves for not meditating enough, for being distracted during practice, or for not experiencing the benefits of mindfulness as quickly as we'd like.

To counteract self-criticism and judgement, cultivate an attitude of self-compassion and kindness towards yourself. Treat yourself with the same warmth and understanding that you would offer to a dear friend who is struggling. Remember that mindfulness practice is a journey, and it's natural to encounter obstacles along the way. Be patient with yourself and celebrate your efforts, no matter how small.

4. Monkey Mind: Racing Thoughts and Mental Chatter

The term "monkey mind" refers to the restless, unsettled nature of the mind, characterized by racing thoughts, mental chatter, and incessant distraction. When practicing mindfulness, we may find it challenging to quiet the mind and focus our attention on the present moment.

To tame the monkey mind, try using anchoring techniques such as focusing on the breath or repeating a mantra. Whenever you notice your mind wandering, gently guide your attention back to your chosen anchor, without judgment or frustration. Remember that the goal of mindfulness practice is not to eliminate thoughts altogether but to cultivate awareness of them and develop a more balanced relationship with our mental landscape.

5. Inconsistency and Lack of Motivation

Consistency is key in mindfulness practice, but many of us struggle to maintain a regular routine amidst the demands of daily life. We may find ourselves skipping meditation sessions or neglecting mindfulness exercises when we're feeling tired, busy, or unmotivated.

To overcome inconsistency and lack of motivation, try setting realistic goals and creating a supportive environment for your practice. Start small by committing to just a few minutes of mindfulness each day, and gradually increase the duration as you build momentum. Find ways to integrate mindfulness into your daily routine, such as practicing mindfulness while brushing your teeth or waiting in line.

6. Comparison and Expectations

In the age of social media, it's easy to fall into the trap of comparing our mindfulness practice to others and setting unrealistic expectations for ourselves. We may feel discouraged when we see others effortlessly meditating for hours or seemingly achieving enlightenment overnight.

To combat comparison and expectations, remember that mindfulness practice is deeply personal and subjective. Focus on your own journey and progress, rather than comparing yourself to others. Celebrate your unique experiences and insights, and trust that your practice will unfold in its own time and in its own way.

7. Balancing Effort and Surrender

Finally, one of the most nuanced challenges in mindfulness practice is finding the balance between effort and surrender. On one hand, we need to exert effort and discipline to maintain a regular practice and overcome obstacles. On the other hand, we must also cultivate a sense of surrender and acceptance, allowing things to unfold naturally without forcing or striving.

To strike this delicate balance, practice cultivating both diligence and non-striving in your mindfulness practice. Approach your practice with dedication and commitment, but also be willing to let go of expectations and attachments to outcomes. Trust in the process and surrender to the present moment, knowing that true transformation arises from a place of openness and receptivity.

Incorporating Mindfulness into Daily Routines

Incorporating mindfulness into daily routines is essential for integrating the practice into your life beyond formal meditation sessions. By infusing mindfulness into everyday activities, you can cultivate a greater sense of presence, awareness, and well-being throughout your day. In this chapter, we'll explore various ways to incorporate mindfulness into your daily routines, from morning rituals to evening reflections.

Starting Your Day Mindfully: Morning Rituals

Begin your day with a mindful morning routine to set a positive tone for the day ahead. Consider incorporating mindfulness practices such as meditation, deep breathing exercises, or gentle stretching into your morning routine. These practices can help center your mind, calm your nervous system, and prepare you for the challenges and opportunities that lie ahead.

For example, you might start your day with a brief meditation session, focusing on your breath or body sensations for a few minutes before getting out of bed. Alternatively, you could practice a few rounds of conscious breathing while sipping a cup of tea or coffee, savoring each sip mindfully.

Bringing Mindfulness to Daily Activities: Mindful Eating

One powerful way to incorporate mindfulness into your daily routine is through mindful eating. Instead of rushing through meals or eating on autopilot, take the time to savor each bite and fully engage your senses in the eating experience. Notice the colors, textures, and flavors of your food, and pay attention to the sensations of chewing and swallowing.

Try to eat slowly and mindfully, chewing each bite thoroughly and pausing between bites to check in with your hunger and fullness cues. Avoid distractions such as screens or reading material while eating, and instead focus on the present moment and the experience of nourishing your body.

Mindful Movement: Exercise and Physical Activity

Physical activity offers an excellent opportunity to practice mindfulness and cultivate awareness of your body and breath. Whether you're going for a walk, practicing yoga, or engaging in a workout routine, approach your physical activity with mindfulness and intention.

Focus on the sensations of movement in your body, noticing the rhythm of your breath, the feeling of your muscles engaging, and the connection between your body and the environment around you. If you're practicing yoga, pay attention to the alignment of your body and the quality of your breath as you move through each posture.

Mindful Work: Bringing Awareness to the Workplace

The workplace is another area where mindfulness can be incorporated into daily routines. Whether you're working from home or in an office setting, take moments throughout the day to pause, breathe, and check in with yourself.

Practice short mindfulness exercises, such as mini-meditations or mindful breathing breaks, to recenter your mind and reduce stress. Set boundaries around technology use to minimize distractions and create space for focused work. Additionally, cultivate a sense of gratitude and appreciation for the work you're doing, recognizing the value and impact of your contributions.

Mindful Transitions: Creating Moments of Pause

Incorporate mindfulness into transitional moments throughout your day to create a sense of rhythm and flow. Pause briefly between activities to take a few conscious breaths and ground yourself in the present moment.

For example, before transitioning from work to leisure activities in the evening, take a few moments to reflect on your day and set intentions for how you want to spend your free time. Similarly, before going to bed, engage in a short mindfulness practice such as a body scan or loving-kindness meditation to promote relaxation and prepare for sleep.

Cultivating Mindful Relationships: Connecting with Others

Finally, bring mindfulness into your interactions with others to foster deeper connections and communication. Practice active listening, paying full attention to the speaker without interrupting or formulating responses in your mind. Approach conversations with curiosity and openness, suspending judgment and cultivating empathy for the other person's perspective.

Additionally, cultivate gratitude and appreciation for the people in your life, recognizing their contributions and expressing heartfelt thanks whenever possible. By infusing mindfulness into your relationships, you can strengthen bonds, enhance communication, and foster a greater sense of connection and belonging.

Incorporating mindfulness into daily routines is a powerful way to cultivate presence, awareness, and well-being in your life. By embracing mindfulness in activities such as morning rituals, eating, movement, work, transitions, and relationships, you can create a more mindful and fulfilling way of living. Experiment with different practices and find what works best for you, adjusting as needed to suit your preferences and lifestyle. Remember that mindfulness is not about perfection but rather about cultivating a gentle awareness and acceptance of the present moment, whatever it may hold.

Setting Realistic Goals for Your Practice

Incorporating mindfulness into your daily routines can be transformative, but like any new endeavor, it's important to approach it with realistic expectations and goals. Setting achievable objectives for your mindfulness practice can help you stay motivated and track your progress over time. In this section, we'll explore how to set realistic goals for your mindfulness practice and provide tips for staying committed to your journey of self-discovery and well-being.

Understanding the Purpose of Goal Setting

Before diving into goal setting for your mindfulness practice, it's helpful to understand the purpose behind it. Goals serve as guideposts, providing direction and motivation for your practice. They help you clarify what you hope to achieve and create a roadmap for getting there. By setting realistic and achievable goals, you can maintain momentum and focus, even when faced with challenges or setbacks.

Identifying Your Motivation

The first step in setting realistic goals for your mindfulness practice is to identify your motivation. What drew you to mindfulness in the first place? What do you hope to gain from your practice? Whether it's reducing stress, improving focus, or cultivating a greater sense of inner peace, clarifying your motivations can help you set goals that align with your values and aspirations.

For example, if your primary motivation for practicing mindfulness is to reduce stress, your goals might focus on incorporating mindfulness techniques into your daily routine to help manage stress more effectively. Or if you're seeking greater self-awareness and personal growth, your goals might involve deepening your meditation practice and exploring mindfulness in various aspects of your life.

Setting SMART Goals

When setting goals for your mindfulness practice, it can be helpful to use the SMART criteria:

- Specific: Clearly define what you want to achieve. Instead of setting a vague goal like "be more mindful," specify how you will practice mindfulness, such as "meditate for 10 minutes every morning."
- Measurable: Make your goals measurable so you can track your progress over time. For example, you might set a goal to increase your meditation sessions from three times a week to five times a week.
- Achievable: Set goals that are realistic and attainable given your current circumstances and resources. It's important to challenge yourself, but not to the point of overwhelming yourself or setting yourself up for failure.
- Relevant: Ensure that your goals are relevant to your overall objectives and motivations for practicing mindfulness. Focus on areas that will have the greatest impact on your well-being and personal growth.
- Time-bound: Set deadlines or milestones for achieving your goals to create a sense of urgency and accountability. This can help prevent procrastination and keep you focused on making progress.

Examples of Realistic Goals

Here are some examples of realistic goals you might set for your mindfulness practice:

- Meditate for 10 minutes every morning before starting your day.
- Practice mindful eating by savoring each bite and eating without distractions at least once a day.
- Take five mindful breaths whenever you feel stressed or overwhelmed throughout the day.
- Attend a weekly mindfulness or meditation class to deepen your practice and connect with a supportive community.

Staying Committed to Your Practice

Once you've set realistic goals for your mindfulness practice, the key is to stay committed and consistent in your efforts. Here are some tips for staying on track:

- Start small: Break your goals down into smaller, manageable steps and gradually build up over time. This can help prevent burnout and make your practice feel more sustainable.
- Create a routine: Incorporate mindfulness into your daily routine by scheduling time for practice each day. Consistency is key

to forming new habits and making lasting changes.
- Stay flexible: Be willing to adapt your goals and practices as needed based on your changing circumstances and experiences. What works for you today may not work tomorrow, and that's okay.
- Practice self-compassion: Be gentle and patient with yourself as you navigate your mindfulness journey. It's normal to experience ups and downs along the way, so be kind to yourself and celebrate your progress, no matter how small.

By setting realistic goals for your mindfulness practice and staying committed to your journey, you can cultivate greater presence, awareness, and well-being in your life. Remember that progress takes time and effort, but the rewards are well worth it.

4. Mindful Work Habits

Techniques for Integrating Mindfulness into Daily Work Life

Incorporating mindfulness into your daily work life can help you navigate the challenges of the modern workplace with greater ease and resilience. By cultivating mindfulness practices tailored to the demands of your job, you can enhance focus, reduce stress, and foster a more positive and productive work environment. In this section, we'll explore various techniques for integrating mindfulness into your daily work life, empowering you to thrive in your professional endeavors.

Mindful Breathing

One of the simplest and most accessible mindfulness techniques for the workplace is mindful breathing. Taking a few moments throughout the day to focus on your breath can help center your mind, calm your nervous system, and reduce stress.

Here's a simple mindful breathing exercise you can try:

- Find a quiet and comfortable place to sit or stand.
- Close your eyes or soften your gaze.
- Take a few deep breaths, inhaling deeply through your nose and exhaling slowly through your mouth.
- Gradually bring your attention to the sensation of your breath as it enters and leaves your body.
- Notice the rise and fall of your chest or the sensation of air passing through your nostrils.
- If your mind wanders, gently bring your focus back to your breath without judgment.

Practicing mindful breathing for just a few minutes can help you feel more grounded and present, even in the midst of a hectic workday.

Mindful Work Breaks

Taking regular breaks throughout the workday is essential for maintaining focus, productivity, and overall well-being. Instead of mindlessly scrolling through your phone or checking social media during breaks, try incorporating mindfulness practices into your downtime.

For example, you might take a short walk outside and focus on the sensations of walking—the feeling of your feet on the ground, the movement of your body, the sights and sounds around you. Or you could practice a brief seated meditation, focusing on your breath or body sensations for a few minutes to relax and recharge.

By using work breaks as opportunities for mindfulness, you can return to your tasks feeling refreshed, rejuvenated, and ready to tackle the challenges ahead.

Mindful Communication

Mindful communication is another powerful technique for integrating mindfulness into your daily work life. By bringing awareness to your interactions with colleagues, clients, and supervisors, you can cultivate deeper connections, improve collaboration, and reduce conflict.

Here are some tips for practicing mindful communication in the workplace:

- Listen actively: Give your full attention to the speaker, maintaining eye contact and nodding or using verbal cues to show that you're engaged.
- Pause before responding: Take a moment to pause and collect your thoughts before responding to questions or comments. This can help you respond more

thoughtfully and avoid reacting impulsively.
- Practice empathy: Put yourself in the other person's shoes and try to understand their perspective, even if you disagree with them. Approach conversations with an open mind and a genuine desire to connect.
- Use nonverbal cues: Pay attention to your body language and facial expressions during conversations. Nonverbal cues can communicate a lot of information, so strive to maintain open and welcoming body language.

By incorporating mindful communication practices into your interactions with others, you can foster a more positive and supportive work environment for yourself and those around you.

Mindful Task Management

Finally, mindfulness can be applied to how you approach and manage your daily tasks and responsibilities. Instead of rushing through tasks mindlessly or multitasking to get everything done, try approaching each task with focused attention and intention.

Here are some tips for practicing mindful task management:

- Prioritize your tasks: Take a few moments at the beginning of each day to identify your top priorities and focus on completing them first. This can help reduce feelings of overwhelm and increase productivity.
- Break tasks into smaller steps: Break larger tasks into smaller, more manageable steps to make them feel less daunting. Focus on completing one step at a time, giving each step your full attention and effort.
- Single-task mindfully: Instead of trying to juggle multiple tasks at once, focus on completing one task at a time with your full attention. This can help improve focus, efficiency, and the quality of your work.
- Take breaks between tasks: Give yourself short breaks between tasks to rest and recharge. Use these breaks to practice mindful breathing, stretch your body, or take a quick walk to clear your mind.

By approaching your tasks with mindfulness and intention, you can increase your productivity, reduce stress, and find greater satisfaction and fulfillment in your work.

Incorporating mindfulness into your daily work life doesn't have to be complicated or time-consuming. By integrating simple mindfulness techniques into your routine, you can enhance focus, reduce stress, and foster a more positive and productive work environment for yourself and those around you. Experiment with different techniques and find what works best for you, adjusting as needed to suit your preferences and the demands of your job. With practice and persistence, you can cultivate a greater sense of presence, awareness, and well-being in your professional endeavors.

Cultivating Focus and Presence at Work

In today's fast-paced work environment, distractions abound, making it challenging to maintain focus and presence throughout the day. However, cultivating these qualities is essential for productivity, creativity, and overall well-being in the workplace. In this section, we'll explore techniques for cultivating focus and presence at work, empowering you to harness your full potential and thrive in your professional endeavors.

Minimize Distractions

One of the first steps in cultivating focus and presence at work is to minimize distractions in your environment. Identify common sources of distraction, such as email notifications, social media, or noisy coworkers, and take steps to reduce their impact on your concentration.

For example, you might turn off email notifications and designate specific times during the day to check and respond to emails. Consider using noise-canceling headphones or finding a quiet corner of the office to minimize distractions from surrounding conversations. By creating a more conducive work environment, you can enhance your ability to stay focused and present throughout the day.

Practice Single-Tasking

Contrary to popular belief, multitasking is not an effective way to get things done. Instead of trying to juggle multiple tasks at once, practice single-tasking by focusing on one task at a time with your full attention.

Set aside dedicated blocks of time for focused work, free from interruptions and distractions. During these periods, immerse yourself fully in the task at hand, giving it your undivided attention until it's completed or until it's time to take a break.

For example, if you're working on a project or report, carve out a specific time slot on your calendar to devote solely to that task. Turn off notifications, close unnecessary tabs or windows on your computer, and commit to focusing on the task until the time is up.

Use Mindfulness Techniques

Mindfulness techniques can be powerful tools for cultivating focus and presence at work. Incorporate mindfulness practices such as mindful breathing, body scans, or short meditation breaks into your daily routine to help anchor your attention and cultivate a greater sense of presence.

For example, you might take a few moments before starting a new task to ground yourself in the present moment by focusing on your breath or sensations in your body. Alternatively, you could practice a brief mindfulness meditation during your lunch break to recharge and reset your mind for the afternoon ahead.

Set Clear Goals and Priorities

Having clear goals and priorities can help you stay focused and present at work by providing a sense of direction and purpose. Take the time to clarify your objectives for the day or week ahead, breaking them down into smaller, actionable steps.

Use tools such as to-do lists, project management software, or time-blocking techniques to organize your tasks and allocate time for focused work on high-priority items. By setting clear goals and priorities, you can avoid feeling overwhelmed and ensure that your time and energy are directed towards activities that align with your objectives.

Take Regular Breaks

While it may seem counterintuitive, taking regular breaks throughout the workday can actually enhance your focus and presence when you return to your tasks. Breaks allow your brain to rest and recharge, reducing mental fatigue and preventing burnout.

Experiment with different types of breaks to see what works best for you. You might take short, frequent breaks to stretch your legs and clear your mind, or longer breaks to engage in activities that help you relax and recharge, such as going for a walk outside or practicing mindfulness meditation.

Practice Gratitude

Finally, cultivating gratitude can help cultivate focus and presence at work by shifting your focus from what's lacking to what's already present. Take a few moments each day to reflect on the things you're grateful for, whether it's supportive colleagues, interesting projects, or simply having a job that allows you to pursue your passions and interests.

By cultivating an attitude of gratitude, you can foster a positive mindset and cultivate a greater sense of presence and appreciation for the opportunities and experiences that come your way.

Cultivating focus and presence at work is a skill that takes time and practice to develop, but the benefits are well worth the effort. By minimizing distractions, practicing single-tasking, using mindfulness techniques, setting clear goals and priorities, taking regular breaks, and cultivating gratitude, you can enhance your ability to stay focused, engaged, and present throughout the workday. Experiment with different techniques and strategies to find what works best for you, adjusting as needed to suit your preferences and the demands of your job. With persistence and dedication, you can cultivate a greater sense of clarity, productivity, and well-being in your professional endeavors.

Mindful Time Management Strategies

Effective time management is essential for success in both professional and personal life. By incorporating mindfulness into your approach to time management, you can enhance your productivity, reduce stress, and cultivate a greater sense of balance and well-being. In this section, we'll explore mindful time management strategies to help you make the most of your time and energy.

Set Priorities Mindfully

Begin by identifying your most important tasks and priorities for the day. Take a moment to reflect on your goals and values, and consider how each task aligns with them. By setting priorities mindfully, you can ensure that your time and energy are directed towards activities that are truly meaningful and impactful.

One helpful technique for setting priorities is the Eisenhower Matrix, which categorizes tasks based on their urgency and importance. Tasks are divided into four quadrants: urgent and important, important but not urgent, urgent but not important, and neither urgent nor important. Focus on tackling tasks in the first two quadrants first, as they have the greatest impact on your goals and priorities.

Practice Time Blocking

Time blocking is a technique that involves allocating specific blocks of time for different tasks and activities throughout the day. Rather than letting your day unfold haphazardly, take control of your schedule by blocking out time for focused work, meetings, breaks, and personal activities.

Start by identifying your most productive times of day and scheduling your most important tasks during those periods. Block out dedicated time for focused work, free from distractions and interruptions. Remember to include breaks in your schedule to rest and recharge, as well as time for personal activities and self-care.

Stay Present and Focused

In today's hyper-connected world, it's easy to become distracted and lose focus. Mindfulness can help you stay present and focused on the task at hand, allowing you to work more efficiently and effectively.

Practice single-tasking by giving your full attention to one task at a time, rather than trying to juggle multiple tasks simultaneously. Minimize distractions by turning off notifications, closing unnecessary tabs or windows on your computer, and creating a conducive work environment.

When you find your mind wandering or becoming overwhelmed, take a moment to pause and refocus. Use mindfulness techniques such as mindful breathing or grounding exercises to anchor your attention in the present moment and bring your focus back to the task at hand.

Set Realistic Expectations

Be realistic about what you can accomplish in a given day and set realistic expectations for yourself. Avoid overcommitting or trying to do too much at once, as this can lead to feelings of overwhelm and burnout.

Break larger tasks down into smaller, more manageable steps, and focus on completing one step at a time. Celebrate your progress and accomplishments along the way, no matter how small, and be kind to yourself if things don't go as planned.

Practice Self-Compassion

Finally, practice self-compassion as you navigate your time management journey. Recognize that time management is a skill that takes time and practice to develop, and be gentle with yourself as you learn and grow.

If you find yourself becoming overwhelmed or stressed, take a step back and practice self-care. Take breaks when needed, engage in activities that help you relax and recharge, and seek support from friends, family, or colleagues if necessary.

By incorporating mindful time management strategies into your daily routine, you can enhance your productivity, reduce stress, and cultivate a greater sense of balance and well-being. Experiment with different techniques and strategies to find what works best for you, and remember to approach your time management journey with patience, persistence, and self-compassion.

Creating a Mindful Workspace Environment

Crafting a mindful workspace environment is essential for fostering focus, productivity, and well-being in the workplace. By intentionally designing your workspace to support mindfulness practices, you can create a conducive environment for concentration, creativity, and overall job satisfaction. In this section, we'll explore various strategies for creating a mindful workspace environment that promotes mental clarity, reduces stress, and enhances overall productivity.

Declutter Your Space

One of the first steps in creating a mindful workspace environment is to declutter your physical space. A cluttered workspace can lead to mental clutter and distractions, making it difficult to stay focused and productive.

Take some time to declutter your desk, removing any unnecessary items or papers that are not actively being used. Keep only the essentials within arm's reach, such as your computer, notebook, and a few pens. Store other items out of sight in drawers or storage bins to maintain a clean and organized workspace.

Organize with Intention

In addition to decluttering, organizing your workspace with intention can help create a more mindful environment. Arrange your desk and office supplies in a way that promotes efficiency and ease of use.

For example, keep frequently used items within easy reach and organize them in a logical manner. Use storage solutions such as file organizers, trays, and shelves to keep your workspace tidy and organized. By creating a visually pleasing and functional workspace, you can enhance your ability to focus and stay on task throughout the day.

Incorporate Natural Elements

Bringing elements of nature into your workspace can help create a calming and grounding environment conducive to mindfulness. Consider adding plants, natural light, or nature-inspired decor to your workspace to promote a sense of tranquility and connection with the natural world.

Plants not only add aesthetic appeal to your workspace but also help purify the air and reduce stress. Choose low-maintenance plants such as succulents or pothos that thrive in indoor environments and require minimal care. Position them near your desk or workspace to enjoy their benefits throughout the day.

Create Zones for Different Activities

Another strategy for creating a mindful workspace environment is to create zones for different activities within your workspace. Designate specific areas for focused work, meetings, brainstorming sessions, and relaxation breaks to optimize productivity and well-being.

For example, set up a comfortable seating area with cozy chairs or cushions for relaxation and reflection. Create a separate area for meetings or collaborative work with a table and chairs conducive to discussion and brainstorming. By delineating different zones within your workspace, you can enhance efficiency, creativity, and overall workflow.

Minimize Digital Distractions

In today's digital age, it's easy to get overwhelmed by constant notifications, emails, and messages. Minimizing digital distractions in your workspace is essential for promoting mindfulness and maintaining focus.

Take steps to limit distractions by silencing notifications, turning off unnecessary devices, and establishing designated times for checking emails and messages. Consider using productivity tools or apps that block distracting websites or apps during focused work sessions. By creating a digital detox zone within your workspace, you can cultivate a more mindful and productive work environment.

Personalize Your Space

Finally, don't forget to personalize your workspace to reflect your personality and interests. Adding personal touches such as photos, artwork, or meaningful objects can help create a sense of comfort and familiarity, making your workspace feel more inviting and inspiring.

Choose decor items that resonate with you and bring you joy, whether it's a favorite quote, a photo of loved ones, or a piece of artwork that inspires creativity. Surrounding yourself with meaningful objects can help create a sense of belonging and connection in your workspace, enhancing your overall well-being and job satisfaction.

By implementing these strategies for creating a mindful workspace environment, you can cultivate a space that supports focus, productivity, and well-being in the workplace. Experiment with different techniques and design elements to find what works best for you, adjusting as needed to suit your preferences and the demands of your job. With a mindful workspace environment, you can create an optimal setting for success and fulfillment in your professional endeavors.

5. Managing Stress and Anxiety

Strategies for Coping with Workplace Stressors

In today's fast-paced and demanding work environments, it's not uncommon to encounter various stressors that can take a toll on your well-being and performance. From tight deadlines to challenging projects to interpersonal conflicts, workplace stressors are an inevitable part of professional life. However, how you respond to these stressors can significantly impact your overall job satisfaction and productivity. In this section, we'll explore strategies for coping with workplace stressors effectively, empowering you to navigate challenges with resilience and grace.

Identify Your Stressors

The first step in coping with workplace stressors is to identify the specific factors that are causing stress in your work environment. Take some time to reflect on the situations, tasks, or interactions that tend to trigger stress for you.

For example, you might find that tight deadlines, high workloads, or conflicts with colleagues are common sources of stress. By pinpointing the specific stressors you're facing, you can develop targeted strategies for managing them more effectively.

Practice Stress Management Techniques

Once you've identified your stressors, it's essential to develop a toolkit of stress management techniques to help you cope with them more effectively. There are many different techniques you can try, so it's essential to experiment and find what works best for you.

Some common stress management techniques include:

- Mindfulness meditation: Taking a few minutes each day to practice mindfulness meditation can help calm your mind, reduce stress, and increase resilience.
- Deep breathing exercises: Practicing deep breathing exercises can help activate your body's relaxation response, reducing feelings of stress and anxiety.
- Progressive muscle relaxation: This technique involves tensing and then relaxing different muscle groups in your body, helping to release tension and promote relaxation.
- Physical activity: Engaging in regular physical activity, such as walking, jogging, or yoga, can help reduce stress levels and improve overall well-being.

Set Boundaries

Setting boundaries is essential for protecting your well-being and preventing burnout in the workplace. Establish clear boundaries around your time, energy, and resources, and communicate them assertively with your colleagues and supervisors.

For example, you might set limits on how late you're willing to work each day or establish guidelines for responding to work emails outside of office hours. By setting boundaries, you can create a more balanced and sustainable approach to work, reducing feelings of overwhelm and stress.

Seek Support

Don't hesitate to reach out for support when you're feeling stressed or overwhelmed at work. Whether it's a trusted colleague, a supportive supervisor, or a professional counselor, having a support system in place can make a significant difference in how you cope with workplace stressors.

Talk to someone you trust about what you're experiencing and explore possible solutions together. Sometimes, simply having someone to listen can help alleviate feelings of stress and provide valuable perspective on the situation.

Practice Self-Care

Self-care is essential for maintaining your well-being and resilience in the face of workplace stressors. Make time for activities that nourish your body, mind, and spirit, even when you're busy with work.

This could include activities such as:

- Getting enough sleep
- Eating a balanced diet
- Exercising regularly
- Spending time with loved ones
- Engaging in hobbies or leisure activities

Prioritizing self-care can help replenish your energy, reduce stress levels, and increase your ability to cope with workplace challenges effectively.

Focus on What You Can Control

Finally, focus on what you can control in your work environment, rather than getting caught up in things beyond your control. While you may not be able to change external circumstances or the behavior of others, you can control how you respond to them.

For example, instead of dwelling on a challenging project or a difficult colleague, focus on what steps you can take to address the situation constructively. This might involve breaking the project down into smaller tasks, seeking clarification from your colleague, or practicing self-compassion and acceptance.

By focusing on what you can control, you can empower yourself to take proactive steps to manage workplace stressors effectively and cultivate a greater sense of resilience in the face of adversity.

Mindfulness Tools for Dealing with Anxiety

Anxiety is a common experience in the workplace, especially in high-pressure environments or during periods of change and uncertainty. While it's normal to feel anxious from time to time, chronic or excessive anxiety can significantly impact your well-being and performance. Fortunately, mindfulness offers a variety of tools and techniques to help manage anxiety effectively. In this section, we'll explore mindfulness tools for dealing with anxiety in the workplace, empowering you to cultivate greater calm, clarity, and resilience in the face of stress.

Mindful Breathing

One of the simplest and most powerful mindfulness tools for managing anxiety is mindful breathing. Mindful breathing involves bringing your full attention to the sensation of your breath as it moves in and out of your body. By focusing on your breath, you can anchor yourself in the present moment and calm your mind and body.

To practice mindful breathing, find a quiet place where you won't be disturbed for a few minutes. Sit comfortably with your feet flat on the floor and your hands resting on your lap. Close your eyes if it feels comfortable, or soften your gaze.

Begin by taking a few deep breaths, inhaling through your nose and exhaling through your mouth. Then, allow your breath to return to its natural rhythm, without trying to control it. Bring your attention to the sensation of your breath as it enters and leaves your body, noticing the rise and fall of your chest or the sensation of air passing through your nostrils.

If your mind starts to wander or you become distracted by anxious thoughts, simply notice this without judgment and gently bring your focus back to your breath. Continue to breathe mindfully for a few minutes, allowing yourself to relax and unwind.

Body Scan Meditation

Another helpful mindfulness tool for managing anxiety is the body scan meditation. Body scan meditation involves systematically bringing your attention to different parts of your body, noticing any sensations or tension you may be holding, and allowing yourself to relax and release it.

To practice a body scan meditation, find a comfortable position either sitting or lying down. Close your eyes and take a few deep breaths to settle into your body. Then, starting at your feet, bring your attention to the sensations in your toes, the soles of your feet, and the tops of your feet. Notice any sensations of warmth, tingling, or tension, without trying to change them.

Continue to move your attention slowly up through your body, scanning each part from your feet to your legs, hips, abdomen, chest, arms, hands, neck, and head. Notice any areas of tension or discomfort, and see if you can soften and release them with each exhale.

As you practice the body scan meditation, you may notice a sense of relaxation and ease spreading throughout your body, helping to alleviate feelings of anxiety and tension.

Mindful Movement

Engaging in mindful movement practices such as yoga or tai chi can also be helpful for managing anxiety in the workplace. These practices combine gentle movement with breath awareness, helping to calm the nervous system and promote relaxation.

Consider taking short breaks throughout the workday to stretch, move your body, and practice mindfulness. This could be as simple as standing up and doing a few gentle stretches at your desk, or taking a walk outside to connect with nature and clear your mind.

By incorporating mindful movement into your daily routine, you can reduce feelings of anxiety and stress, improve your mood and energy levels, and enhance your overall well-being.

Mindful Self-Compassion

Finally, practicing mindful self-compassion can be a powerful tool for managing anxiety in the workplace. Mindful self-compassion involves treating yourself with kindness and understanding, especially during times of difficulty or distress.

When you notice feelings of anxiety arising, try to bring a sense of gentle curiosity and compassion to your experience. Acknowledge your feelings without judgment, and remind yourself that it's normal to feel anxious from time to time.

Offer yourself words of kindness and support, just as you would to a friend or loved one experiencing similar struggles. You might say to yourself, "May I be kind to myself in this moment," or "May I find peace and ease amidst the challenges of the day."

By cultivating mindful self-compassion, you can create a sense of safety and security within yourself, reducing feelings of anxiety and promoting emotional resilience in the face of workplace stressors.

Recognizing and Managing Triggers

In the realm of mindfulness and stress management, recognizing and managing triggers is a crucial skill. Triggers are external events, situations, or circumstances that elicit a stress response or negative emotional reaction. By becoming aware of these triggers and learning how to manage them effectively, you can cultivate greater resilience and well-being in both your personal and professional life.

Identifying Triggers

The first step in managing triggers is to identify them. Triggers can vary widely from person to person and may include specific situations, people, tasks, or even physical sensations. Pay attention to moments when you notice a shift in your mood, energy level, or stress level, as these may indicate the presence of a trigger.

For example, you might notice that you feel anxious or irritable every time you have a meeting with a particular colleague, or that you feel overwhelmed whenever you receive a new assignment with a tight deadline. By identifying these triggers, you can begin to explore their underlying causes and develop strategies for managing them more effectively.

Exploring Underlying Patterns

Once you've identified your triggers, take some time to explore the underlying patterns and dynamics at play. Ask yourself questions such as:

- What specific aspects of this situation or event trigger my stress or negative emotions?
- Are there any past experiences or traumas that may be contributing to my reaction?
- Do I have any underlying beliefs or assumptions that are influencing how I perceive and respond to this trigger?

- Are there any patterns or recurring themes in my triggers that I can identify?

By gaining insight into the underlying patterns and dynamics of your triggers, you can begin to address them more effectively and develop targeted strategies for managing them.

Developing Coping Strategies

Once you have a better understanding of your triggers, work on developing coping strategies to manage them more effectively. This might include techniques such as:

- Mindfulness meditation: Using mindfulness techniques to stay present and grounded when you encounter a trigger.
- Deep breathing exercises: Using deep breathing exercises to calm your nervous system and reduce the intensity of your stress response.
- Cognitive reframing: Challenging negative thoughts and beliefs associated with your triggers and replacing them with more positive and adaptive perspectives.
- Setting boundaries: Establishing clear boundaries to protect yourself from triggers or reduce their impact on your well-being.

- Seeking support: Reaching out to friends, family, or a professional counselor for support and guidance in managing your triggers.

Experiment with different coping strategies to see what works best for you, and be patient with yourself as you navigate this process.

Creating a Supportive Environment

Finally, create a supportive environment that helps minimize the impact of triggers on your well-being. Surround yourself with people who understand and respect your boundaries, and cultivate a work environment that promotes open communication, collaboration, and mutual respect.

By creating a supportive environment and developing effective coping strategies, you can learn to recognize and manage triggers more effectively, leading to greater resilience and well-being in both your personal and professional life.

Building Resilience Through Mindfulness

Mindfulness is not only a tool for managing stress and anxiety but also a powerful means of building resilience. Resilience is the ability to bounce back from challenges, setbacks, and adversity with strength and flexibility. By cultivating mindfulness practices, you can enhance your resilience and navigate life's ups and downs with greater ease and grace.

Cultivating Present-Moment Awareness

At the heart of resilience-building through mindfulness is the practice of cultivating present-moment awareness. Mindfulness teaches us to be fully present and engaged with whatever is happening in the here and now, without getting caught up in worries about the past or future.

By learning to anchor ourselves in the present moment, we can develop greater clarity, focus, and perspective, even in the face of adversity. This allows us to respond to challenges with greater skill and resilience, rather than reacting impulsively or getting overwhelmed by stress.

Acceptance and Non-Judgment

Mindfulness also teaches us the importance of acceptance and non-judgment. Instead of resisting or denying difficult emotions or experiences, mindfulness encourages us to acknowledge them with kindness and compassion.

When we accept our experiences without judgment, we create space for growth and healing. We learn to respond to challenges with greater resilience, recognizing that setbacks and failures are a natural part of life's journey.

Cultivating Self-Compassion

Self-compassion is another essential aspect of resilience-building through mindfulness. Self-compassion involves treating ourselves with kindness and understanding, especially during times of difficulty or distress.

When we practice self-compassion, we recognize that we are human beings deserving of love and compassion, just like everyone else. We offer ourselves the same warmth and care that we would offer to a dear friend or loved one, nurturing our inner resilience and well-being.

Adapting to Change

Mindfulness also helps us adapt to change more effectively, another key aspect of resilience. Life is full of unexpected twists and turns, and the ability to adapt and adjust to new circumstances is essential for building resilience.

By cultivating mindfulness, we learn to embrace change with openness and curiosity, rather than fear or resistance. We develop greater flexibility and adaptability, allowing us to navigate life's transitions with grace and resilience.

Cultivating Gratitude

Finally, mindfulness can help cultivate gratitude, which is closely linked to resilience. Gratitude involves recognizing and appreciating the positive aspects of our lives, even in the midst of challenges and difficulties.

By practicing gratitude, we shift our focus away from what's lacking or wrong and towards what's right and good. This helps build our resilience by fostering a sense of hope, optimism, and appreciation for the abundance in our lives.

Overall, mindfulness is a powerful tool for building resilience and navigating life's challenges with strength, grace, and resilience. By cultivating present-moment awareness, acceptance, self-compassion, adaptability, and gratitude, we can enhance our resilience and thrive in the face of adversity.

6. Enhancing Communication and Relationships

Improving Interactions with Colleagues and Managers

Effective communication and positive relationships with colleagues and managers are essential for success in the workplace. Mindfulness can play a valuable role in enhancing these interactions by promoting empathy, active listening, and emotional intelligence.

Practicing Active Listening

One way mindfulness can improve interactions with colleagues and managers is by enhancing our ability to engage in active listening. Active listening involves fully focusing on what the other person is saying without interrupting or jumping to conclusions. It requires being present in the moment and truly understanding the speaker's perspective.

By practicing mindfulness, we can cultivate the skills needed for active listening. We learn to quiet our minds and set aside distractions, allowing us to give our full attention to the speaker. This not only fosters better understanding and rapport but also helps build trust and respect in our professional relationships.

Cultivating Empathy

Mindfulness also helps cultivate empathy, the ability to understand and share the feelings of others. When we approach interactions with colleagues and managers from a place of empathy, we are better able to connect with them on a deeper level and respond to their needs and concerns with compassion and understanding.

By practicing mindfulness, we can develop greater awareness of our own emotions and experiences, which allows us to better empathize with the experiences of others. This fosters stronger bonds and more meaningful relationships in the workplace, leading to improved collaboration and teamwork.

Managing Emotions Effectively

Another way mindfulness can enhance interactions with colleagues and managers is by helping us manage our own emotions effectively. Mindfulness teaches us to observe our thoughts and feelings without judgment, allowing us to respond to challenging situations with greater clarity and composure.

When we are mindful of our emotions, we are better able to regulate them and prevent them from negatively impacting our interactions with others. This promotes more positive and constructive communication, even in the face of conflict or disagreement.

Fostering Positive Communication

Mindfulness also fosters positive communication by promoting openness, honesty, and authenticity. When we approach interactions with colleagues and managers with a mindful attitude, we are more likely to speak and act in ways that are genuine and sincere.

By practicing mindfulness, we can develop greater self-awareness and insight into our communication patterns and habits. This allows us to communicate more effectively, express ourselves clearly and assertively, and build stronger, more trusting relationships with our colleagues and managers.

Overall, mindfulness can be a powerful tool for improving interactions with colleagues and managers in the workplace. By practicing active listening, cultivating empathy, managing emotions effectively, and fostering positive communication, we can create a more supportive and harmonious work environment where everyone can thrive.

Building Trust and Rapport in the Workplace

Trust and rapport are the foundation of strong and successful relationships in the workplace. When colleagues trust and respect each other, they can collaborate more effectively, communicate openly, and achieve shared goals. Mindfulness can play a key role in fostering trust and rapport by promoting authenticity, empathy, and positive communication.

Authenticity and Transparency

One of the cornerstones of building trust and rapport is authenticity. Being genuine and transparent in your interactions with colleagues creates an environment of openness and honesty, where people feel comfortable being themselves and expressing their thoughts and feelings.

Mindfulness encourages authenticity by fostering self-awareness and acceptance. When you approach interactions with colleagues from a mindful perspective, you are more likely to communicate honestly and openly, without fear of judgment or criticism.

Empathy and Understanding

Empathy is another essential component of building trust and rapport in the workplace. By understanding and empathizing with the perspectives and experiences of others, colleagues can forge deeper connections and build stronger relationships.

Mindfulness cultivates empathy by encouraging individuals to be present and attentive to the experiences of others. When you practice mindfulness, you develop the ability to listen actively, observe without judgment, and respond with compassion and understanding.

Positive Communication

Positive communication is vital for building trust and rapport in the workplace. Clear, respectful, and constructive communication fosters mutual respect and understanding among colleagues, laying the groundwork for strong and productive working relationships.

Mindfulness promotes positive communication by helping individuals communicate more effectively and assertively. When you approach interactions with colleagues mindfully, you are better able to express yourself clearly and assertively, while also listening actively and empathetically to others.

Consistency and Reliability

Consistency and reliability are essential for building trust and rapport in the workplace. Colleagues need to know that they can rely on each other to follow through on commitments, meet deadlines, and fulfill responsibilities.

Mindfulness can help individuals cultivate consistency and reliability by promoting focus, accountability, and resilience. When you practice mindfulness, you develop the ability to stay present and focused on the task at hand, even in the face of distractions or challenges. This allows you to consistently deliver high-quality work and uphold your commitments to colleagues.

Building Connections and Collaboration

Ultimately, trust and rapport are essential for building connections and fostering collaboration in the workplace. When colleagues trust and respect each other, they are more likely to collaborate effectively, share ideas openly, and support each other's success.

Mindfulness promotes connection and collaboration by fostering a sense of community and shared purpose among colleagues. When individuals approach interactions with mindfulness, they create a supportive and inclusive work environment where everyone feels valued and respected.

In conclusion, mindfulness can be a powerful tool for building trust and rapport in the workplace. By promoting authenticity, empathy, positive communication, consistency, and collaboration, mindfulness helps create a culture of trust and respect where colleagues can thrive and succeed together.

Mindful Listening and Effective Communication

Effective communication is the cornerstone of successful relationships, both personally and professionally. Mindful listening is a powerful practice that can enhance communication skills, deepen understanding, and strengthen relationships in the workplace.

Presence and Attention

At the heart of mindful listening is presence and attention. When you engage in mindful listening, you give your full focus and attention to the speaker, without allowing your mind to wander or become distracted by internal thoughts or external stimuli.

For example, imagine you're in a team meeting discussing a new project. Instead of thinking about what you're going to say next or checking your phone for messages, you focus entirely on what your colleague is saying. You listen attentively to their ideas, observe their body language, and acknowledge their perspective without judgment or interruption.

Empathy and Understanding

Mindful listening also fosters empathy and understanding. By truly listening to others without judgment or preconceived notions, you create a space for them to express themselves authentically and feel understood and valued.

For instance, suppose a colleague approaches you to discuss a challenge they're facing in their work. Instead of rushing to offer solutions or dismiss their concerns, you practice mindful listening. You listen with empathy, acknowledging their feelings and validating their experiences, which helps them feel heard and supported.

Clarity and Response

Furthermore, mindful listening promotes clarity and thoughtful response. When you listen mindfully, you gain a deeper understanding of the speaker's message, allowing you to respond in a more meaningful and constructive way.

For instance, suppose you're in a brainstorming session with your team, and a colleague shares an innovative idea. Instead of immediately critiquing or dismissing their suggestion, you practice mindful listening. You take a moment to reflect on their idea, ask clarifying questions, and offer constructive feedback, which encourages further dialogue and collaboration.

Tips for Mindful Listening:

Practice active listening by maintaining eye contact, nodding, and providing verbal and nonverbal cues to show you're engaged.

Avoid interrupting or interjecting while the speaker is talking. Instead, wait for natural pauses to ask questions or offer input.

Focus on the speaker's words, tone, and body language, rather than getting distracted by your own thoughts or external distractions.

Cultivate empathy and understanding by putting yourself in the speaker's shoes and trying to see the situation from their perspective.

Take a moment to reflect on the speaker's message before responding, ensuring your response is thoughtful and relevant to the conversation.

In summary, mindful listening is a valuable skill that can enhance effective communication and foster deeper connections in the workplace. By practicing presence, empathy, and clarity in your interactions with colleagues, you can cultivate a culture of respect, understanding, and collaboration.

Resolving Conflict Through Mindfulness

Conflict is a natural part of any workplace environment, but how it is managed can significantly impact team dynamics and productivity. Mindfulness offers a valuable approach to resolving conflict by promoting self-awareness, emotional regulation, and open communication.

Self-Awareness and Emotional Regulation

One of the first steps in resolving conflict through mindfulness is cultivating self-awareness and emotional regulation. By becoming more aware of our own thoughts, emotions, and reactions, we can better understand the underlying causes of conflict and respond more skillfully.

For example, suppose you find yourself in a disagreement with a colleague during a team meeting. Instead of reacting impulsively or defensively, you pause and take a moment to notice your thoughts and emotions. You acknowledge any feelings of frustration or anger without judgment and then choose how to respond thoughtfully and calmly.

Empathy and Understanding

Mindfulness also fosters empathy and understanding, which are essential for resolving conflict effectively. By actively listening to the perspectives of others and trying to see the situation from their point of view, we can build empathy and create a foundation for mutual respect and collaboration.

For instance, imagine you're mediating a conflict between two team members who have differing opinions on a project approach. Instead of taking sides or dismissing their concerns, you practice mindful listening. You encourage each person to express their perspective without interruption and validate their feelings, which helps them feel heard and understood.

Open Communication and Collaboration

Mindfulness encourages open communication and collaboration, which are crucial for resolving conflict constructively. By creating a safe space for dialogue and sharing perspectives, teams can work together to find mutually beneficial solutions to conflicts.

For example, suppose there's tension between two departments over resource allocation. Instead of escalating the conflict or avoiding the issue, team leaders facilitate a mindful discussion where each side can express their needs and concerns openly. Through respectful communication and a willingness to compromise, the teams find a solution that meets the needs of both parties.

Tips for Resolving Conflict Through Mindfulness:

1. Take a mindful pause: When conflict arises, take a moment to pause and center yourself before responding.
2. Practice active listening: Listen attentively to the perspectives of others without judgment or interruption.
3. Cultivate empathy: Try to understand the feelings and motivations of others involved in the conflict.

4. Focus on solutions: Instead of dwelling on past grievances, focus on finding constructive solutions that meet the needs of all parties.
5. Foster a culture of mindfulness: Encourage mindfulness practices such as meditation and reflection within your team or organization to support conflict resolution efforts.

7. Work-Life Integration

Balancing Professional Responsibilities with Personal Well-Being

Maintaining a balance between professional responsibilities and personal well-being is essential for overall happiness and success. In today's fast-paced work environments, it can be challenging to find this balance, but mindfulness offers valuable strategies for navigating this delicate equilibrium.

Setting Boundaries

One of the first steps in balancing professional responsibilities with personal well-being is setting boundaries. Establishing clear boundaries between work and personal life helps prevent burnout and allows for time to recharge and focus on self-care.

For example, consider implementing boundaries such as not checking work emails after a certain time in the evening or setting aside designated "off" days where work-related tasks are avoided. By delineating specific times for work and personal activities, individuals can create a sense of structure and balance in their lives.

Prioritizing Self-Care

Prioritizing self-care is another crucial aspect of balancing professional responsibilities with personal well-being. Engaging in activities that promote physical, emotional, and mental health is essential for maintaining resilience and preventing burnout.

Examples of self-care activities include regular exercise, adequate sleep, mindfulness meditation, spending time with loved ones, pursuing hobbies and interests, and seeking support from friends or a therapist when needed. By prioritizing self-care, individuals can replenish their energy reserves and approach work with renewed focus and clarity.

Practicing Mindful Time Management

Mindful time management is a valuable skill for balancing professional responsibilities and personal well-being. By consciously allocating time to different tasks and activities, individuals can optimize productivity while also ensuring they have time for rest and relaxation.

For instance, consider using time-blocking techniques to schedule specific periods for focused work, breaks, and self-care activities throughout the day. Additionally, practicing mindfulness during work tasks can help individuals stay present and focused, reducing distractions and enhancing productivity.

Maintaining Perspective

Maintaining perspective is crucial for balancing professional responsibilities with personal well-being. While work is undoubtedly important, it's essential to remember that personal health and happiness are equally valuable.

For example, if faced with a demanding work project or deadline, individuals can practice mindfulness to stay grounded and maintain perspective. By recognizing that work is just one aspect of life and that personal well-being should not be sacrificed for professional success, individuals can navigate challenges with greater resilience and balance.

Seeking Support

Finally, seeking support from colleagues, friends, or mentors can be instrumental in balancing professional responsibilities with personal well-being. Opening up about challenges and seeking advice or encouragement from others can provide valuable perspective and help individuals feel less isolated in their struggles.

In summary, balancing professional responsibilities with personal well-being requires intentionality, self-awareness, and mindfulness. By setting boundaries, prioritizing self-care, practicing mindful time management, maintaining perspective, and seeking support, individuals can achieve a harmonious balance between work and personal life.

Setting Boundaries and Prioritizing Self-Care

Setting boundaries and prioritizing self-care are essential practices for maintaining well-being and preventing burnout in today's busy world. By establishing clear boundaries around work and personal life and making self-care a priority, individuals can create a healthier and more balanced lifestyle.

Setting Boundaries

Setting boundaries involves defining limits and guidelines for how we interact with work and other aspects of our lives. This could include setting specific work hours, designating times when work-related communication is off-limits, and establishing boundaries around personal time and space.

For example, suppose you typically find yourself responding to work emails late into the evening, leading to feelings of stress and burnout. In that case, you might decide to set a boundary of not checking work emails after a certain time each day. By clearly communicating this boundary to colleagues and sticking to it consistently, you create space for relaxation and rejuvenation outside of work hours.

Prioritizing Self-Care

Prioritizing self-care involves intentionally making time for activities that nourish and rejuvenate our bodies, minds, and spirits. This could include practices such as exercise, meditation, spending time with loved ones, pursuing hobbies, and getting adequate rest.

For instance, suppose you have a busy work schedule that often leaves little time for self-care activities. In that case, you might decide to prioritize self-care by scheduling regular exercise sessions, setting aside time for relaxation and leisure activities, and ensuring you get enough sleep each night. By making self-care a non-negotiable part of your routine, you invest in your overall well-being and resilience.

Tips for Setting Boundaries and Prioritizing Self-Care:

1. **Communicate your boundaries**: Clearly communicate your boundaries to colleagues, friends, and family members, so they understand your needs and respect your limits.
2. **Learn to say no**: Practice saying no to requests or commitments that don't align with your priorities or values, freeing up time and energy for activities that matter most.
3. **Schedule self-care**: Block out time in your schedule for self-care activities, treating them with the same level of importance as work-related tasks.
4. **Listen to your body**: Pay attention to your body's signals and honor its need for rest, relaxation, and nourishment.
5. **Practice self-compassion**: Be kind to yourself and recognize that it's okay to prioritize your well-being over productivity or external expectations.

In summary, setting boundaries and prioritizing self-care are essential practices for maintaining balance and well-being in today's fast-paced world. By establishing clear boundaries around work and personal life and making self-care a priority, individuals can cultivate a healthier and more sustainable lifestyle.

Strategies for Creating a Healthy Work-Life Balance

Achieving a healthy work-life balance is crucial for overall well-being and satisfaction. It involves finding a harmonious equilibrium between professional responsibilities and personal life, allowing individuals to thrive in both domains. Here are some effective strategies for creating and maintaining a healthy work-life balance:

1. **Define Your Priorities**: Take time to clarify your values and priorities, both in your career and personal life. Determine what matters most to you and allocate your time and energy accordingly. By aligning your actions with your values, you can create a more fulfilling and balanced life.

2. **Set Boundaries**: Establish clear boundaries between work and personal life to prevent one from encroaching on the other. This could include setting specific work hours, designating technology-free zones at home, and creating guidelines for when and how you engage in work-related tasks outside of office hours.

3. **Practice Time Management**: Effective time management is essential for balancing competing demands and maximizing productivity. Use tools such as calendars, to-do lists, and time-blocking techniques to organize your tasks and prioritize

your activities. Be realistic about what you can accomplish in a given day and learn to delegate or say no to tasks that aren't essential.

4. **Schedule Regular Breaks**: Incorporate regular breaks into your daily routine to rest and recharge. Taking short breaks throughout the day can help prevent burnout, boost productivity, and improve overall well-being. Use breaks to engage in activities that promote relaxation and stress relief, such as going for a walk, practicing mindfulness, or simply stepping away from your work environment.

5. **Cultivate Mindfulness**: Mindfulness practices, such as meditation and deep breathing exercises, can help cultivate awareness and presence in the moment. Incorporate mindfulness into your daily routine to reduce stress, increase resilience, and enhance your ability to cope with challenges. Even just a few minutes of mindfulness each day can make a significant difference in your overall well-being.

6. **Prioritize Self-Care**: Make self-care a non-negotiable part of your routine by prioritizing activities that nourish your body, mind, and spirit. This could include exercise, healthy eating, getting enough sleep, spending time with loved ones, and pursuing hobbies and interests outside of work. Remember that self-care isn't selfish; it's essential for maintaining your health and happiness.

7. **Learn to Unplug**: In today's hyper-connected world, it's easy to feel tethered to work at all times. Make a conscious effort to disconnect from work-related technology during your downtime, whether it's evenings, weekends, or vacations. Set boundaries around when and how you engage with work-related communication to protect your personal time and mental well-being.

8. **Seek Support**: Don't hesitate to reach out for support from friends, family, or colleagues when needed. Surround yourself with a supportive network of individuals who understand the importance of work-life balance and can offer encouragement, advice, and perspective.

Incorporating these strategies into your daily life can help you achieve a healthier and more balanced approach to work and personal life, leading to greater satisfaction and well-being.

Mindfulness Practices for Enhancing Personal Relationships

Mindfulness isn't just beneficial for individual well-being; it can also enhance the quality of personal relationships by promoting presence, empathy, and communication. Incorporating mindfulness practices into your interactions with others can deepen connections, foster understanding, and cultivate healthier relationships. Here are some mindfulness practices for enhancing personal relationships:

1. **Active Listening**: Practice active listening during conversations by giving your full attention to the speaker without judgment or distraction. Focus on what the person is saying, without formulating your response in your mind or interrupting. Use nonverbal cues such as nodding and maintaining eye contact to show that you're engaged and attentive.

Example: When your partner is sharing their thoughts or feelings with you, put down your phone, turn off the TV, and give them your undivided attention. Listen with an open heart and mind, allowing them to express themselves fully without interruption.

2. **Cultivate Empathy**: Cultivate empathy by putting yourself in the other person's shoes and trying to understand their perspective and emotions. Practice empathy by acknowledging and validating the other person's feelings, even if you don't agree with them. This can help build trust and strengthen emotional bonds in relationships.

Example: If a friend expresses sadness or frustration about a challenging situation, acknowledge their feelings by saying something like, "It sounds like you're going through a tough time. I'm here for you if you need to talk." Show empathy by offering support and validation without trying to fix their problems.

3. **Nonjudgmental Communication**: Practice nonjudgmental communication by expressing yourself honestly and authentically while remaining open and nonreactive to the other person's responses. Avoid criticizing or blaming the other person and instead focus on expressing your thoughts and feelings with kindness and respect.

Example: Instead of saying, "You always forget to do your share of the chores," try saying, "I've noticed that I've been feeling overwhelmed with the housework lately. Can we talk about finding a more balanced approach to dividing tasks?"

4. **Mindful Conflict Resolution**: Approach conflicts with mindfulness by staying present and calm during disagreements. Take a pause when emotions run high to breathe and collect your thoughts before responding. Practice active listening and empathy to understand the other person's perspective and work together to find a resolution that honors both parties' needs and feelings.

Example: During a disagreement with a family member, take a few deep breaths to center yourself and calm your emotions. Listen to their concerns without interrupting, and express your own thoughts and feelings in a calm and respectful manner. Work together to find common ground and solutions that address both perspectives.

5. **Gratitude Practice**: Cultivate gratitude in relationships by expressing appreciation for the people you care about and the positive aspects of your interactions. Take time each day to reflect on the things you're grateful for in your relationships and express your gratitude openly and sincerely.

Example: Before bed, take a moment to think about three things you appreciate about your partner or a close friend. Share your gratitude with them by sending a text message, writing a note, or simply expressing your thanks in person.

By incorporating these mindfulness practices into your personal relationships, you can deepen connections, foster understanding, and cultivate greater happiness and fulfillment in your interactions with others.

8. Sustaining Your Mindfulness Practice

Tips for Maintaining Consistency and Motivation

Consistency and motivation are key factors in establishing and maintaining a mindfulness practice. However, staying consistent and motivated can sometimes be challenging, especially when life gets busy or distractions arise. Here are some tips to help you maintain consistency and motivation in your mindfulness practice:

1. **Establish a Routine**: Set aside dedicated time each day for your mindfulness practice and integrate it into your daily routine. Whether it's first thing in the morning, during your lunch break, or before bed, having a consistent time for practice can help make it a regular habit.

Example: If you decide to practice mindfulness meditation, carve out 10-15 minutes each morning before starting your day. Create a peaceful environment free from distractions, such as turning off your phone and finding a quiet space where you won't be interrupted.

2. **Start Small**: Begin with manageable goals and gradually increase the duration or intensity of your practice over time. Starting small can help prevent overwhelm and increase the likelihood of sticking with your practice long-term.

Example: If you're new to mindfulness, start with just a few minutes of practice each day and gradually increase the duration as you become more comfortable. Focus on consistency rather than trying to achieve perfection.

3. **Find Accountability**: Share your mindfulness goals with a friend, family member, or mindfulness buddy who can help keep you accountable and provide support and encouragement along the way. Knowing that someone else is counting on you can increase motivation and make it easier to stay consistent.

Example: Partner with a friend who also wants to establish a mindfulness practice. Check in with each other regularly to share your progress, discuss challenges, and offer support and encouragement.

4. **Mix It Up**: Keep your mindfulness practice fresh and engaging by exploring different techniques and approaches. Experiment with mindfulness meditation, mindful movement,

breathwork, or other mindfulness activities to find what resonates best with you.

Example: If you find sitting meditation challenging, try a walking meditation or a body scan practice instead. Explore different mindfulness apps, books, or courses to discover new techniques and insights.

5. **Set Realistic Expectations**: Be gentle with yourself and set realistic expectations for your mindfulness practice. Understand that there will be days when your practice feels effortless and days when it feels more challenging. Embrace the ebb and flow of your practice without judgment or self-criticism.

Example: If you miss a day of practice or your mind wanders during meditation, acknowledge it with kindness and compassion. Remember that mindfulness is about cultivating awareness and acceptance of the present moment, including the ups and downs of your practice.

By implementing these tips, you can maintain consistency and motivation in your mindfulness practice, leading to greater well-being and fulfillment in your life.

Overcoming Setbacks and Challenges

In any mindfulness practice, setbacks and challenges are inevitable. Whether it's difficulty maintaining focus during meditation, facing unexpected stressors, or falling out of your routine, encountering obstacles is a natural part of the journey. However, it's how you respond to these challenges that can make all the difference in your practice. Here are some strategies for overcoming setbacks and challenges in your mindfulness practice:

1. **Cultivate Self-Compassion**: Approach setbacks with kindness and compassion towards yourself. Recognize that setbacks are a normal part of the learning process and that you're not alone in facing challenges. Treat yourself with the same level of understanding and support that you would offer to a friend in a similar situation.

Example: If you miss a day of meditation or find it difficult to stay present during practice, remind yourself that it's okay to have off days. Offer yourself words of encouragement and remind yourself of your commitment to your well-being.

2. **Reframe Challenges as Opportunities**: Instead of viewing challenges as obstacles to your practice, reframe them as opportunities for

growth and learning. Every setback presents a chance to gain insight into yourself, deepen your understanding of mindfulness, and strengthen your resilience.

Example: If you encounter difficulty staying focused during meditation, see it as an opportunity to practice bringing your attention back to the present moment with gentleness and patience. Each time you redirect your focus, you're strengthening your mindfulness muscle.

3. **Adjust Your Approach**: If you find that a particular aspect of your mindfulness practice isn't working for you, don't be afraid to adjust your approach. Experiment with different techniques, durations, or times of day to find what resonates best with you. Flexibility and adaptability are key to overcoming challenges.

Example: If sitting meditation feels uncomfortable or inaccessible, try incorporating mindfulness into everyday activities such as walking, eating, or washing dishes. Find ways to integrate mindfulness seamlessly into your daily life.

4. **Seek Support**: Don't hesitate to reach out for support when facing challenges in your mindfulness practice. Whether it's through a

meditation group, online community, or trusted mentor, connecting with others who share similar experiences can provide valuable encouragement, guidance, and perspective.

Example: Join a local meditation group or online mindfulness community where you can share your experiences, ask questions, and receive support from fellow practitioners. Having a sense of community can make it easier to navigate challenges and stay motivated in your practice.

5. **Practice Gratitude**: Cultivate gratitude for the opportunity to engage in mindfulness practice and for the lessons learned through challenges. Shift your focus from what's lacking to what you're grateful for in your practice, acknowledging the progress you've made and the insights gained along the way.

Example: Take a moment each day to reflect on the benefits of your mindfulness practice and express gratitude for the opportunity to cultivate greater awareness, presence, and well-being in your life.

By applying these strategies, you can navigate setbacks and challenges with resilience and grace, ultimately deepening your mindfulness practice and reaping the benefits in your daily life.

Celebrating Progress and Successes

Amidst the journey of mindfulness practice, it's crucial to acknowledge and celebrate the progress and successes you achieve along the way. Cultivating a sense of appreciation for your growth can fuel your motivation and reinforce your commitment to your practice. Here are some ways to celebrate your progress and successes in mindfulness:

1. **Reflect on Your Growth**: Take time to reflect on how far you've come since beginning your mindfulness journey. Notice the changes in your awareness, presence, and overall well-being. Celebrate the small victories, such as moments of clarity during meditation or instances where you responded to stress with greater resilience.

Example: Reflect on how your ability to stay present has improved over time. Notice moments in your daily life where you're able to bring mindfulness to challenging situations and respond with greater calmness and clarity.

2. **Acknowledge Your Efforts**: Recognize the effort and dedication you've invested in your mindfulness practice. Acknowledge the commitment it takes to show up regularly, even when faced with obstacles or distractions. Give yourself credit for prioritizing your well-being and taking proactive steps towards personal growth.

Example: Acknowledge the time and energy you've dedicated to your practice, whether it's through daily meditation, mindful movement, or integrating mindfulness into your daily routines. Celebrate your commitment to nurturing your mental and emotional health.

3. **Set Milestones and Celebrate Achievements**: Establish milestones or goals for your mindfulness practice and celebrate when you reach them. Whether it's completing a certain number of consecutive days of meditation, deepening your understanding of a mindfulness technique, or experiencing a breakthrough in your practice, take time to acknowledge and celebrate your achievements.

Example: Set a goal to meditate for 30 consecutive days and celebrate when you reach this milestone. Treat yourself to something special or engage in a self-care activity to honor your dedication and perseverance.

4. Share Your Successes: Share your progress and successes with others who support and encourage your mindfulness journey. Celebrate your achievements with friends, family, or members of your mindfulness community. Sharing your experiences can amplify the sense of joy and fulfillment you feel and inspire others to embark on their own mindfulness journey.

Example: Share your experiences and insights from your mindfulness practice with a close friend or family member. Celebrate your growth together and offer support and encouragement to one another on your respective paths.

5. Cultivate Gratitude: Cultivate gratitude for the positive changes and benefits that mindfulness has brought into your life. Take a moment each day to express gratitude for the opportunities for growth, the insights gained, and the moments of peace and clarity you experience through your practice.

Example: Practice a gratitude meditation where you reflect on the blessings in your life and express appreciation for the gift of mindfulness. Notice how cultivating gratitude enhances your sense of well-being and connection to yourself and others.

By celebrating your progress and successes in mindfulness, you can reinforce your commitment to your practice and cultivate a deeper sense of joy, fulfillment, and gratitude in your life.

Cultivating a Lifelong Mindfulness Habit

Building a lifelong mindfulness habit requires dedication, patience, and a willingness to embrace the practice as a fundamental part of your daily life. Here are some strategies to help you cultivate a sustainable mindfulness habit that lasts a lifetime:

1. **Start Small and Be Consistent**: Begin by incorporating short mindfulness practices into your daily routine, such as a five-minute meditation or mindful breathing exercise. Consistency is key to establishing a habit, so commit to practicing mindfulness regularly, even if it's just for a few minutes each day.

Example: Start your day with a brief mindfulness practice, such as a mindful breathing exercise, before you get out of bed. Set aside a few minutes each morning to focus on your breath and cultivate a sense of calm and presence for the day ahead.

2. **Integrate Mindfulness into Daily Activities**: Look for opportunities to infuse mindfulness into your everyday activities, such as mindful eating, walking, or even washing dishes. By bringing mindful awareness to mundane tasks, you can turn them into opportunities for presence and self-reflection.

Example: Practice mindful eating by savoring each bite of your meals and paying attention to the flavors, textures, and sensations of the food. Notice how mindful eating enhances your enjoyment of the meal and fosters a deeper connection to your body's signals of hunger and fullness.

3. **Set Intentions for Your Practice**: Clarify your reasons for practicing mindfulness and set clear intentions for what you hope to gain from the practice. Whether it's reducing stress, enhancing focus, or cultivating compassion, having a sense of purpose can motivate you to stay committed to your mindfulness habit.

Example: Reflect on why you're drawn to mindfulness and what you hope to achieve through your practice. Write down your intentions and revisit them regularly to reaffirm your commitment to your mindfulness journey.

4. **Embrace Imperfection and Learn from Challenges**: Understand that mindfulness is a lifelong journey, and there will be ups and downs along the way. Instead of striving for perfection, embrace imperfection as a natural part of the process and an opportunity for growth. Learn from challenges and setbacks, and use them as opportunities to deepen your understanding of yourself and your practice.

Example: Notice when your mind wanders during meditation or when you encounter resistance to practicing mindfulness. Instead of judging yourself harshly, approach these moments with curiosity and compassion. Use them as opportunities to explore the patterns of your mind and cultivate greater self-awareness.

5. **Stay Connected to Your Why**: Regularly remind yourself of the benefits of mindfulness and how it aligns with your values and goals. Stay connected to your "why" to maintain motivation and enthusiasm for your practice, even when faced with obstacles or distractions.

Example: Take time to reflect on the positive changes you've experienced as a result of your mindfulness practice, such as increased resilience, greater clarity, or improved relationships. Use these reflections as reminders of why mindfulness is important to you and how it contributes to your overall well-being.

By incorporating these strategies into your daily life, you can cultivate a lifelong mindfulness habit that nourishes your mind, body, and spirit and enhances your quality of life for years to come.

Printed in Great Britain
by Amazon